The Royal Palace

6-WEEK BIBLE STUDY
M.E. MAYORGA

5 SISTERS MINISTRY

BRISBANE, AUSTRALIA

The Royal Palace: 6 Week Bible Study

Copyright © 2023 M.E. Mayorga

Published by 5 Sisters Ministry

P.O. BOX 6505, Upper Mt Gravatt, QLD Australia 4122

This title is also available as an eBook.

Visit www.gigistorylibrary.com.au

ISBN: 978-0-6454319-6-4

All rights reserved. No part of this publication may be reproduced, stored, or transmitted in any form, except for brief quotations in printed reviews, without written permission of the publisher.

Editing: Debbie Cosier

Cover image: Depositphoto.com

Scripture quotations marked (NIV) are taken from the Holy Bible, New International Version®, NIV®. Copyright © 1973, 1978, 1984, 2011 by Biblica, Inc.™ Used by permission of Zondervan. All rights reserved worldwide, www.zondervan.com. The "NIV" and "New International Version" are trademarks registered in the United States Patent and Trademark Office by Biblica, Inc.™

Dear reader,

Have you ever read about the royal women of the Bible? There are quite a few women but, in this study, you will look at six.

Anisenath—Benevolent Princess of the Nile

Zaria—Purposeful Queen of Sheba

Jezebel—Idolatrous Queen of Israel

Jehosheba—Fearless Princess of Judah

Esther—Courageous Queen of Persia

Salome—Seductress Princess of Jerusalem

We believe that starting with God every morning will set you up for a great day. Instead of reaching for your phone as soon as you open your eyes, why not reach for this study guide, and spend ten minutes in His Word?

Your heart will no longer be filled with anxiety. The peace of God will surround you. If you're not in the habit of having morning worship, give this a try for the next six weeks and see how it goes.

Why not study this book with a friend or with a group of girls once a week? It will not only be fun, but it will also help you process ideas and answer questions that come up as you study together.

A Few Tips

Before using this book as your morning devotional, there are a few things you need to do:

1. Space—Find a quiet place and set it up for 'just-you-and-God' time, away from the kitchen, siblings, television, and noise. You will concentrate so much better and experience the peace you need. Play soft instrumental music and light a scented candle. Grab a hot chocolate, tea, or smoothie, and enjoy your morning.

2. Material—You will need a Bible (digital or paper), pens, pencils, highlighters and erasers.

3. Alarm—Set your alarm for fifteen minutes before your usual wake-up time so you can spend at least ten minutes in His Word before you start your day.

4. Prayer—Ask God to help you get up on time and give you the desire to spend time with Him. Ask the Holy Spirit to fill you with wisdom.

Have your space, materials, and journal ready to go before you go to bed. Pack your school bag and make sure your uniform is ready, so you don't panic about running late.

I hope you enjoy this book and can feel the peace that God wants you to have.

Hugs,

M.E. Mayorga

6-Week Study Chart

Tick each day you complete an activity.

WEEKS	DAYS						
	Monday	Tuesday	Wednesday	Thursday	Friday	Saturday/Sunday	TOTAL DAYS
Week 1							
Week 2							
Week 3							
Week 4							
Week 5							
Week 6							

Evaluate

How did you do this past six weeks? _____

Did you miss any days? How many? _____

How many days in total did you study? _____

Remember: It's never too late. Go back and finish the days you haven't completed.

Content

WEEK 1	Compassion	Anisenath—Benevolent Princess of the Nile........1
WEEK 2	Purpose	Zaria—Purposeful Queen of Sheba......................29
WEEK 3	Idolatry	Jezebel—Idolatrous Queen of Israel....................55
WEEK 4	Resilience	Jehosheba—Fearless Princess of Judah............83
WEEK 5	Courage	Esther—Courageous Queen of Persia............107
WEEK 6	Peer Pressure	Salome—Seductress Princess of Jerusalem..133

Answer Page...161

About the Author...165

Week One

Anisenath
Benevolent Princess of the Nile

"Compassion is to look beyond your pain, to see the pain of others."

Yasmin Mogahed

Monday

"Therefore, as God's chosen people, holy and dearly loved, clothe yourselves with compassion, kindness, humility, gentleness and patience." Colossians 3:12

This week: You are looking at Anisenath, the Egyptian princess who saved baby Moses from capture and death.

Personal attribute: The princess showed *compassion*—a lovely characteristic to develop, making you more loving towards those who are suffering.

Definition of compassion: A strong feeling of sympathy and sadness for the suffering or bad luck of others and a wish to help them (dictionary.cambridge.org)

In this week's study, you will look at parts of Princess Anisenath's story and short stories of girls your age.

Story

> The sound of a whip and a scream echoed through the morning, and she jumped. Up ahead, she noticed the slaves at work. An Egyptian taskmaster was beating a young man.
>
> "You are being lazy! Work harder or you will bleed to death," the Egyptian bellowed.
>
> The young man was hunched over waiting for the next whip lash to hit his back.
>
> "Get me closer," Anisenath ordered her carriers.
>
> The men moved her closer, and just as the Egyptian was about to hit the Hebrew again, Anisenath lifted her hand and shouted, "Is that the way to treat a man who is unarmed?"

At the sound of her voice, the stout taskmaster's head shot up. Immediately, he prostrated himself to the dusty ground. "Princess Anisenath!" His voice and bulbous stomach shook.

"I believe it is unjust to hit a young man who has no weapon to defend himself. I command you to let him go!" She felt her voice rise a few notes.

"But... my lady, he was sleeping on the job. We need to get these monuments erected in due time. Your father, our great god Pharaoh, has given us a time frame." The man remained on the ground with droplets of sweat on his bald head.

"If you resume beating him, he will no longer be able to do his work. You will be one worker less, and my father would have your head for allowing the delay." She almost felt like grinning at her ingenious comeback.

The slave master's mouth dropped. "Of course, my lady." He struggled to his feet, and with perspiration running down his face and chest, he gave orders to the young man to get back to work.

The Hebrew turned to face the princess and inclined his head. Princess Anisenath observed the young man, from his dark, curly head to the bottom of his feet. He did not look older than her twenty years. His body was well sculpted, like the pillars of the temple. He wore a dark loincloth, and she watched as his bare chest heaved with each breath he took. She felt her face heat from staring at the young man's body, but it wasn't out of lust, just curiosity. Everywhere she looked, she saw well-built Hebrews. Muscular and strong. Healthy and crimson cheeked. Even their children looked well. It was as if the gods smiled down at them and blessed them with bodies of the gods themselves. How was that possible? Should they not have protruding bones with pale skin and gaunt faces? They worked as hard as camels, yet they remained strong. She shook her head as the young man bowed and ran toward a group of slaves making bricks.

With one last glance at the young man, she motioned to her manservants to take her home. The taskmaster remained with his head bowed until she disappeared around the corner and lost him in the dust's thickness.

Her heart ached for the slaves, and she hoped that one day when she became Pharaoh, she would eradicate such cruelty. (The Royal Palace pg. 5)

Questions

How does the princess feel when she watches the Hebrew man being beaten?

_____

_____

_____

What would you have done in her situation?

_____

_____

_____

Bible Reading

It's time to open your Bibles so you can read about this kind princess. Her story is found in Exodus.

Read Exodus 2: 5-6 and answer the questions.

Why was the princess at the Nile River?

_____

_____

_____

What did she see?

_____
_____
_____

When the princess saw the baby crying, what did she feel?

_____
_____
_____

Personal Thoughts

Do you think you are compassionate?

_____
_____
_____

Is compassion something you have thought about before?

_____
_____
_____

Is compassion something you would like to develop?

___

Pray

Spend a few minutes in silent prayer or write out your prayer below.

___

Tuesday

Story

Sophie is in year 10 and goes to a medium-size school. She loves her school but notices something that bothers her. Around the school, there are too many students on their own at lunchtime. They have no friends to hang out with. She feels sorry for them. One day, she talks to her mum about it and her mum advises her to pray and see what she can come up with to help change the situation. Two weeks later, she has a brilliant idea. She talks to the chaplains and principal, who like her idea. Sophie implements 'The Lounge,' a classroom that is open during lunchtimes where kids can come and hang around, play boardgames and chat. Teachers and senior students supervise The Lounge and many lonely kids come to hang out and make friends with students in other grades. Sophie is so happy that she has made a small difference in her school.

Is there a need you see in your school, church, or community that weighs heavily on your heart? What could you do about it?

_____

_____

_____

_____

_____

_____

_____

_____

Quiz

Do you think you're a compassionate person? Find out with this short quiz.

During a maths class, you notice one of your friends is looking distracted and upset. You:

    a. Lean over and ask her quietly if she's okay and needs help with the maths' revision questions.
    b. Tell your friend to concentrate on her work or she won't pass her math's exam.
    c. Ignore your friend and let her sort it out. She will tell you when she's ready.

Just before a school play, you notice that the lead girl, who has not been very nice to you in rehearsals, is having a serious case of stage fright. You:

    a. Take her aside and share how you have dealt with stage fright before. Then wish her all the best.
    b. Let one of the drama teachers know so they can speak with her.
    c. Ignore her and concentrate on your own performance. Besides, she's been nasty throughout rehearsals and it serves her right.

You just saw your friend's boyfriend kissing another girl. You:

    a. Break the news as gently as possible to your friend and tell her you're there to support her.
    b. Ring your friend and blurt out the bad news.
    c. Stay quiet. You don't want to hurt her feelings and cause trouble. She can find out on her own.

You're walking around at lunchtime and see two students bullying a younger student. You:

    a. Walk over with your best friend and tell the bullies to stop. You inform the bullies you are telling the teacher.
    b. Walk over to the nearest teacher on duty and let them know.
    c. Walk past as fast as you can. You do not want to get involved and become a target.

Your church has a picnic. You notice that some new people have come, and they have a teen girl around your age. You:

a. Go over and invite her to eat with you and your friends.
b. Tell your Bible study teacher about the new teen girl so she can talk to her.
c. Ignore her. After all, she looks shy, and you don't want to make her more uncomfortable.

You walk past a homeless person on the footpath. You:

a. Buy them something to eat and deliver it to them.
b. Drop a $2 coin you find in your purse and walk off.
c. Turn your face the other way and pretend you're on the phone.

Your church pastor has announced that volunteers are going to help Alice clean her house on Sunday. You:

a. Put your name down and commit to helping for two hours so you also have time to finish your assignments.
b. Put your name down because it makes you look good, but have no plans to help.
c. Refuse to put your name down as Sunday is your day off and you have plans.

Tally: A _____   B _____   C _____

If you scored mostly A, you have a kind heart. You love to help people wherever you can. You don't like to see others hurting or suffering and believe God has put you on this earth to help. One day, you plan to make a big difference in the world.

If you scored mostly B, your kind heart is a work in progress. You have the right idea and want to help, but more 'important' things keep getting in the way. You also feel embarrassed to be seen around people in need. Your heart is a work in progress. There is time to change and develop a heart like Jesus'.

> If you scored mostly C, you have plenty of room to develop a kinder heart! You don't really understand why you should help others and would rather not be seen or associated with people who are 'needy.' You have a reputation to uphold and believe that people should sort out their own problems, they don't need you to do it for them. All of this means that, right now, your heart is not in the right place—but it's never too late to make changes and work through this. If you do even one kind thing a week for another person, you will notice your heart begin to soften.

Which one are you?

_____

_____

_____

Were you surprised at the answer?

_____

_____

_____

How can you become more compassionate if that is something you're lacking?

_____

_____

_____

_____

Personal Thoughts

Aside from fear, age, gender, or money, if there was *one* thing you could change in this world for the better, what would it be?

_____
_____
_____
_____
_____
_____
_____

Pray

Spend a few minutes in silent prayer or write out your prayer below.

_____
_____
_____
_____
_____
_____
_____
_____

Wednesday

Story

Filled with awe, Anisenath stared at the strange basket made of papyrus. By the smell, it seemed to have been coated with tar and pitch. The potent scent itched her delicate nose.

Carefully, she lifted the lid and peered inside. The puckered face of a baby met her eyes, and with an open mouth, the baby began to cry, disturbing the early morning peace.

Anisenath gasped. "It's a baby!" Her throat constricted at the thought of this precious child being in the Nile's crocodile-infested waters. Who would do such a cruel act?

The child continued crying. His tiny hands balled into fists, and his fat little legs were flinging everywhere. He looked about twelve weeks old, with ruddy cheeks and little rolls on his arms. What caught her attention was the cloth, the colour of dust, which covered his body.

"Hebrew!" Anisenath breathed the words, and her eyes widened as she touched the fabric.

Gently, she took hold of one of his chubby hands, and he grabbed and pulled at her thumb. A giggle escaped her lips. The baby was strong, just like all Hebrews. He tightened his grip on her finger. She smiled and leaned her face close to his whimpering one.

"Hello, little one," she whispered. "You are safe now." She ran her free hand over his little forehead and on one side of his face. The gentle touch and soothing words quieted his anxious spirit. He looked at her with alert brown eyes, and he cooed. Anisenath's heart melted. (The Royal Palace pg. 31)

What would you have done in Princess Anisenath's situation?

_____
_____
_____

Have you ever experienced compassion or kindness from someone?

Yes   No

Explain what happened.

_____
_____
_____

Have you ever shown compassion or kindness to someone?

_____
_____
_____

Who was the person and what was their situation?

_____
_____
_____

What did you do?

_____
_____
_____

How did you feel afterward?

_____
_____
_____

Bible Reading

Look at the following verses to see what the bible says about compassion.

Write Ephesians 4:32 in the space below.

_____
_____
_____

Who do you need to show compassion to?

_____
_____
_____

How can you show compassion?

___

Who else forgave you?

___

In 1 John 3:18, there's a great verse. Read it and answer the question.

"Dear children, let us not love with words or speech but with actions and in truth."

How are we to love?

___

Personal Thoughts

What is one compassionate thing you can do today?

___

Pray

Spend a few minutes in silent prayer or write out your prayer below.

Thursday

Story

> Kayla groans, rolls her eyes, and storms up the stairs. Seriously, her parents are so ridiculous! She can't understand what the big deal is about helping at the homeless shelter and feeding people who don't have a home. Why did they write her name down to go? Feeling anger bubbling just under the surface, Kayla yanks open the drawer and jerks out a pair of leggings. Once dressed in her oldest clothes, she makes her way back downstairs. The beep of a car horn makes her jump and she looks through the living room window to see Harper and her parents arrive. They're all going together and she mumbles something about wishing the day was over and catching diseases under her breath as she walks out the front door.

Questions

Why was Kayla so angry to help in the homeless shelter?

_____
_____
_____

What do you honestly think of her attitude?

_____
_____
_____

What would you have done in her situation?

_____

_____

_____

Bible Reading

Write out Proverbs 19:17

_____

_____

_____

Explain what this verse means.

_____

_____

_____

Write out John 15:12

_____

_____

_____

Personal Thoughts

"Compassion is to look beyond your pain, to see the pain of others."

What does this quote by Yasmin Mogahed mean?

_____

_____

_____

What can you do to make a difference in your community or the world?

_____

_____

_____

Pray

Spend a few minutes in silent prayer or write out your prayer below.

_____

_____

_____

_____

_____

_____

Friday

Story

Anisenath watched the woman's face and noticed how her eyes softened and lingered on the sleeping baby. Eyes filled with love? The princess tilted her head to one side. As she opened her mouth to speak, the baby squirmed. His little mouth opened, and he wailed.

"He is hungry." Anisenath uncovered his wriggling body. "I will not make him wait any longer. Please take great care of him." Her eyes filled with tears as she bent over and gave the baby a light kiss on his cheek. She handed him over to Jochebed and watched as the woman welcomed him into her arms. The baby twisted his little head to her chest, and his mouth went straight to Jochebed's breast.

"There, there, little one. I will feed you soon." Jochebed touched his forehead with one finger. Instantly the child stopped crying and looked around until his face met Jochebed's.

Anisenath watched as he cooed and smiled with the Hebrew woman. Love radiated from her face. The familiarity between them was undeniable.

The princess gasped and covered her mouth with her hand. This was the baby's mother! Anisenath wanted to cry with joy. The gods were good; they had reconnected a mother and son. Her son now.

"I have a decree for you to take and keep safe. No soldier can touch him. My father's decree does not affect him." She motioned for Onofria to hand over the paper.

"Miriam, please take hold of that document." Jochebed smiled. "Thank you, my lady. I have no words to express my gratitude for delivering this little boy who was sentenced to death. On behalf of his mother, I thank you."

She watched as the mother touched her son's upper arm and ran her finger over the bracelet.

> "That is a symbol that he belongs to me and he is royal. No hand can be laid upon him."
>
> Jochebed nodded with tears spilling down her face. "May the God of Abraham bless you for your compassion and kindness, and may he shine his face on you today and forever."
>
> Anisenath gaped at the beautiful blessing she had received. Never had words to a god sounded so musical. She inclined her head and smiled. "Thank you." Her voice cracked, and she quickly cleared her throat.
>
> Composing herself, she gave a few more minutes of instructions, kissed the baby goodbye, and watched as Miriam, Jochebed, and the baby left the Egyptian grounds and went to theirs. With their backs toward her, Anisenath let the tears flow freely, her heart yearning to have her baby back. Her only consolation was that he was safe and death could not touch him.
>
> She lifted her eyes to the sky and whispered a thank-you. With one last glance toward the disappearing figures in the distance, Anisenath turned back to her palace and went in search of her father. (The Royal Palace pg. 40)

Jesus on earth

The princess had a lovely and compassionate heart, but there is one person who is the ultimate example of compassion: *Jesus*. While on earth, Jesus did many kind things and helped many.

Bible Reading

Read the story in Matthew 20:29-34 below where Jesus showed compassion.

Two Blind Men Receive Sight

29 As Jesus and his disciples were leaving Jericho, a large crowd followed him.

30 Two blind men were sitting by the roadside, and when they heard that Jesus was going by, they shouted, "Lord, Son of David, have mercy on us!"

31 The crowd rebuked them and told them to be quiet, but they shouted all the louder, "Lord, Son of David, have mercy on us!"

32 Jesus stopped and called them. "What do you want me to do for you?" he asked.

33 "Lord," they answered, "we want our sight."

34 Jesus had compassion on them and touched their eyes. Immediately, they received their sight and followed him.

Do you think Jesus feels his heart move with compassion when he witnesses what is happening in the world today?

Yes   No   Maybe

What things in this world make your heart sad and heavy?

_____

_____

_____

_____

While on earth, Jesus was the ultimate example of compassion. He not only talked about it, but He *showed* it.

1 John 3:18 says, "Dear children, let us not love with words or speech but with actions and in truth."

Pray

Spend a few minutes in silent prayer or write out your prayer below.

_____

_____

_____

_____

_____

_____

Saturday/Sunday

The verse of the week: _____

_____

What did you like/dislike about the woman you studied this week?

What did you learn this week?

Why should you be compassionate?

What's one compassionate thing you can start doing this coming week?

What do you need God to help you with?

Journal

Week Two

Zaria
Purposeful Queen of Sheba

"Use me, God. Show me how to take who I am, who I want to be, and what I can do, and use it for a purpose greater than myself."

– Martin Luther King Jr.

Monday

"Be on your guard; stand firm in the faith; be courageous; be strong." 1 Corinthians 16:13

This week: You are looking at the Queen of Sheba who went to see for herself if King Solomon was truly who they said he was.

Personal attribute: She was assertive, determined, and purposeful in finding out the truth—she was not satisfied with what others told her. She needed to witness his wisdom to herself. Her character trait is purposeful, and you are going to read more about this admirable characteristic.

Definition of purposeful: showing that you know what you want to do or aimed at achieving something; determined. (dictionary.cambridge.org)

In this week's study, you'll look at parts of the Queen of Sheba story and short stories of girls your age.

Story

> Soon they were strolling the garden under her favourite parasol—a gift from her late father. A slight breeze refreshed her face. She was glad she had put her hair up today and worn a simple gown of white with gold and blue fringes.
>
> "As I mentioned before, my lady, the king of the North, has done incredible things for his country. He is not only wise but also extremely wealthy."
>
> "Do you know how Solomon got his wisdom?" She was not sure what intrigued her about this foreign king with his strange ways and unknown God.

> "I do not know. However, I believe it has something to do with the God he believes in."
>
> Zaria pursed her lips. "Do you think... do you think if I ask to meet this king, he would accept an audience with me?"
>
> "My lady?" Jaleel stopped walking and turned to face her.
>
> "It might sound like I have lost my mind, but I wonder if I may visit this man. I could talk to him and discuss the economy of Sheba." Zaria squinted. She liked the idea very much.
>
> "Hmm." Jaleel started walking again. "Why not discuss the economy with me or some of our educated men?"
>
> "Jaleel, I believe you and my advisors are intelligent, and you know many things. There comes a time when one must seek a wider view from someone outside his or her own country." Zaria rubbed her hands together. "It would be a good idea to have an outsider give me a different perspective."
>
> "You make a valid point," Jaleel said. (The Royal Palace pg., 61)

Questions

How does the queen feel about meeting the King of the North?

_____

_____

_____

If you wanted to learn from a person who could teach you, what would you do?

Bible Reading

It's time to open your Bible so you can read about this queen. Her story is found in 1 Kings and 2 Chronicles.

Read 2 Chronicles 9:1-12

Who did the queen meet?

How did the queen feel when she saw everything the king had?

What did she tell King Solomon?

_____

_____

_____

Just like the Queen of Sheba sought Solomon, you are to seek God.
A close relationship with Him will enhance your life.

Personal Thoughts

Do you depend on other people to guide you in your spiritual walk with God? How?

_____

_____

_____

Why is it important for you to develop your own walk with God and not rely on others?

_____

_____

_____

Pray

Spend a few minutes in silent prayer or write out your prayer below.

Tuesday

Story

> Audrey sits in front of the TV, watching a sermon with her family. It's interesting. The pastor is talking about spiritualism and how shows, movies, and books with witchcraft and magic will pull you away from Jesus. Audrey isn't sure if she believes the pastor. After all, she watches a lot of movies about superheroes who have magical powers, yet she still studies her Bible! How is that a bad thing? Besides, the magic in the movies isn't real! Surely, the pastor can't be right. She looks around at her family and notices that everyone is watching and listening intently. Do they have lots of thoughts and questions going around in their minds, too? Do they believe everything he's saying? Her head hurts. Feeling frustrated, she excuses herself and tells her parents she needs to finish an assignment. This is true, but also a great excuse to leave a confusing situation!

Why do you think Audrey was so confused? What bothered her about the situation?

_____

_____

_____

Have you ever questioned pastors, preachers, or people that talk about God or explain facts that confuse you? What happened and what did you do?

_____

_____

_____

Why is it important for you to get clarity if something is confusing you?

_____

_____

_____

God wants you to find Him all the time. He wants you to go to Him just like the Queen of Sheba, when she went seeking King Solomon.

There's a great verse in the Bible that talks about this.

Fill in the blanks of the verse found in Acts 17:27

G_____ _____

Find the verse in another version if you don't understand the meaning.
Try the Easy Read Version (ERV).

What does this verse mean?

_____

_____

_____

God wants you to look for Him and spend time with Him every day.

Personal Thought

What is one thing you can do this week to get to know Jesus on a personal level?

_____

_____

_____

Pray

Spend a few minutes in silent prayer or write out your prayer below.

_____

_____

_____

_____

_____

_____

Wednesday

Story

The king revealed they had a grand banquet prepared for her the next evening, but for today he would give her a tour of the grand palace. Zaria enjoyed everything he showed her. They walked the splendid corridors filled with tapestries depicting battles won. Other paintings on the walls had drawings of King Solomon, and one particular wall in the king's prayer room caught her attention.

The entire room was the colour of the moon—it had minimal furniture and soft cushions in an array of colours scattered across the room.

"This is the prayer room." Solomon's voice held a tone of pride. "It is where we communicate with our God."

Zaria felt the reverence. "I do not see any images of your God." She looked around. The only thing she could see were inscriptions on the walls. Beautifully written in elegant ink.

"Our God is invisible, my lady," Solomon said simply.

Zaria glanced quickly at Jaleel, who looked as perplexed as she felt. "Invisible? I'm intrigued." In her palace, they had many gods according to their needs. The goddess of fertility, the god of war, the god of rain and field, the goddess of love, the god who brought healing. Statues of gold, silver, and ivory adorned every corner in her palace.

"Our God is the most powerful God. The God of the universe. He created nature and humans."

"He sounds grand . . . but why not showcase his greatness for all to see?" She felt confused.

"Our God forbids it. He wants us to love him and communicate with him through prayer. He does not want anything made of gold to represent him. Nothing can

> compare to him." Solomon continued walking around the room and showing the letterings on the wall.
>
> One caught her eye, and she stopped to read it out loud. "The law of the Lord is perfect, refreshing the soul. The statutes of the Lord are trustworthy, making wise the simple. The precepts of the Lord are right, giving joy to the heart. The commands of the Lord are radiant, giving light to the eyes. The fear of the Lord is pure, enduring forever. The decrees of the Lord are firm, and all of them are righteous. They are more precious than gold, than much pure gold; they are sweeter than honey, than honey from the honeycomb."
>
> Queen Zaria exhaled. "Such an exquisite poem."
>
> "My father, David, wrote this. He was a poet and songwriter. He wrote many lyrics about our God." (The Royal Palace pg. 72)

What would you have done in Queen Sheba's situation? What questions would you have asked King Solomon?

_____

_____

_____

_____

List two or three things that confuse you about your religion or God.

_____

_____

_____

Who can you talk to about these concerns?

_____

_____

_____

Why is it important to discuss these with someone?

_____

_____

_____

Bible Reading

Look at the following verse to see what the Bible says about seeking God.

Write Jeremiah 29:13 in the space below.

_____

_____

_____

What does this verse mean?

_____

_____

_____

Personal Thoughts

Do you ever feel bored or unmotivated to spend time with God?

_____
_____
_____

Why do you feel that way?

_____
_____
_____

What steps can you take to change the way you feel?

_____
_____
_____

Pray

Spend a few minutes in silent prayer or write out your prayer below.

Thursday

Story

Scenario 1

Emilee wakes up at 6:00 am on school days. She grabs her Bible and spends five minutes reading and praying to God. She loves the quiet time. It fills her with peace and she has less anxiety.

Scenario 2

Emilee wakes up at 6:30 am. She showers, has breakfast, and goes to school. When school finishes, she goes to soccer practice. She gets home, showers, and has dinner. She cleans the kitchen and helps around the house with some chores. By 7:00 pm she hurries to do homework and then crashes into bed, exhausted.

Questions

Why does Emilee like reading in the mornings?

_____

_____

_____

Why would personal worship time not work for Emilee in the evenings?

_____

_____

_____

The Queen of Sheba had one goal and one purpose. If your one goal and purpose is to find God, you will also discover He is so much more than your parents, teachers, pastors, and friends can convey!

It's great to claim God for yourself instead of simply as an extension of your family tradition.

Bible Reading

Write Psalm 5:3 in the space below.

_____

_____

_____

What does this verse mean?

_____

_____

_____

Why is it important to spend time with God? Why do people make such a big deal about it?

_____

_____

_____

There are a few reasons but today I want to share three:

ONE

Truth: Spending time with God teaches you Truth. You get wisdom and understanding so that you can recognise Satan's lies.

TWO

Peace: Spending time with God will give you peace. Life is often crazy, busy, overwhelming, chaotic, and confusing. In God, you find peace. There is nothing more peaceful than spending time with God in the morning. It sets you up for the day and you feel refreshed and recharged after hanging out with Jesus.

THREE

Connect: Spending time with God gives you a deeper connection with Him. You'll soon see Him as your friend and He will be the first to hear the latest news, greatest celebrations and accomplishments, and biggest disappointments. He will be right there with His arms outstretched, ready to comfort you. Our best friends may let us down, but Jesus NEVER will.

Personal Thoughts

"Use me, God. Show me how to take who I am, who I want to be, and what I can do, and use it for a purpose greater than myself."

What does this quote by Martin Luther King Jr. mean?

_____

_____

_____

What is one thing you can do today to seek God and get closer to Him?

_____

_____

_____

Pray

Spend a few minutes in silent prayer or write out your prayer below.

_____

_____

_____

_____

_____

Friday

Story

One morning, as she was in the garden attempting to talk to Solomon's God, the king sent a message inviting her to join him in the temple for a burnt-offering ceremony. She made haste and prepared herself with fine clothing. It intrigued her to know about this burnt offering he mentioned. The king and his advisor escorted her to a section of the temple. The temple, Solomon explained, had not been finished, but he promised, when it was done, it was going to be the grandest monument ever built. Queen Zaria had absolutely no doubt that it would be as he said. After a prayer and some melodious music, the king, along with the high priest of the temple, set on the altar an animal as a burnt offering to their Lord. As the smoke evaporated into the sky, Zaria listened to the king ask for forgiveness for him and his household. He thanked the Lord and concluded his praises until his sacrifice had disappeared from the altar. Zaria asked him many questions, and he patiently answered each one. Talking to this man made her feel that ruling a kingdom with God was possible. Solomon's God was becoming more appealing to her with each passing day.

After the ceremony, they escorted Zaria to eat a sumptuous breakfast of the finest fruit, nuts, and food she had ever seen. To her delight, Jaleel had been invited as well, and he was in the banquet room talking to other officials when she arrived. She heard him excuse himself from the group and head her way. They stopped in the middle of the room, unaware of their surroundings.

"I have just been to a burnt-offering ceremony held by the king." She felt excited to talk about it. "It was such a solemn moment, and I felt God."

"I have felt God multiple times for the last few days," Jaleel replied. "It is hard to explain the true feeling, but it is like nothing I have ever experienced."

Zaria nodded. "I agree with you, and it makes me want to know him better."

Jaleel's light brown eyes gleamed. "I must confess that I do too."

> Their conversation was interrupted by a servant boy announcing breakfast was served. As Zaria looked around the room, she felt her heart swell with emotion and thankfulness for having made the trip to meet the mysterious King Solomon, who ended up being more than she imagined. (The Royal Palace pg. 77)

Jesus on earth

The queen had a spiritual and purposeful heart, but there is one person who is the ultimate example of spirituality and purpose: *Jesus*. While on earth, Jesus spent a lot of time in connection with His Father. He was purposeful in seeking Him.

Bible Reading

Read the verses found in Matthew 14: 23-25 where Jesus is spending time with His Father.

Jesus Walks on the Water

22 Immediately, Jesus made the disciples get into the boat and go on ahead of him to the other side, while he dismissed the crowd.

23 After he had dismissed them, he went up on a mountainside by himself to pray. Later that night, he was there alone,

24 and the boat was already a considerable distance from land, buffeted by the waves because the wind was against it.

25 Shortly before dawn, Jesus went out to them, walking on the lake.

The Twelve Apostles - Luke 6:12

12 One of those days, Jesus went out to a mountainside to pray and spent the night praying to God.

Jesus Prays in a Solitary Place - Mark 1:35

35 Very early in the morning, while it was still dark, Jesus got up, left the house and went off to a solitary place, where he prayed.

Do you think Jesus wants you to be purposeful in seeking Him today?

Yes   No   Maybe

What overwhelms you about prioritising time with God?

_____

_____

_____

What excites you about prioritising time with God?

_____

_____

_____

While on earth, Jesus gave the ultimate example of leading a purposeful spiritual life. He not only talked about it, but he *demonstrated* it.

Luke 6:12 says, one of those days Jesus *went out to a mountainside to pray* and spent the night praying to God.

Spend a few minutes in silent prayer or write out your prayer below.

Saturday/Sunday

The verse of the week: _____
_____

What did you like/dislike about the woman you studied this week?

What did you learn this week?

Why should you be purposeful in your spiritual life?

If you have doubts about God or other spiritual questions. Who can you talk to about it and when?

What do you need God to help you with?

Journal

Week Three

Jezebel
Idolatrous Queen of Israel

"Idolatry happens when we take good things and make them ultimate things."

Timothy Keller

Monday

"Dear children, keep yourselves from idols." 1 John 5:21

This week: You are looking at Queen Jezebel who was married to King Ahab. She was an evil and idolatrous queen who eliminated anyone against her.

Personal attribute: Her character was idolatrous—a negative character trait where she loved and invested too much time in unimportant things, or 'idols'.

Definition of idolatry: very great admiration or respect for someone, often too great, or the act of praying to a picture or object as part of a religion (dictionary.cambridge.org)

In this week's study, you will look at parts of Queen Jezebel's story and short stories of girls your age.

Story

> She stood and sauntered to sit next to him. She rubbed his back and grinned. "My beloved, is this a way the king of Israel acts?"
>
> He stared at her with a blank look and shook his head.
>
> "Get up and eat! Rejoice." She smirked. "I will get you the vineyard of Naboth." She kissed him and walked over to the desk, sat down, and wrote on the open scroll.
>
> "What are you planning?" He stretched his neck, trying to decipher from where he sat what she was writing.
>
> She did not reply.

He did not ask again; instead, he rubbed his beard, deep in thought.

Jezebel folded the scroll, placed his seal over it, and rang the gong. Elana watched in fascination as a soldier entered from the side door and bowed. Jezebel stretched her arm with the scroll. "Take this to the elders and nobles who live in Naboth's city, and tell them I command they do as this says."

The man took the scroll, bowed, and left the room.

Jezebel rubbed her hands together. A satisfied look registered on her face, her amber eyes slanted and malicious.

Ahab reached for her hand and pulled her with force onto his lap. "What did you write?"

She placed her hand around his neck and leaned her embellished head onto his. "I have proclaimed a day of fasting and have requested they seat Naboth in a prominent place amongst the people so—"

"Prominent?"

She placed her index finger on his lips. "Shh. Once he is seated, two vagabonds will accuse him in front of everyone that he has cursed both God and the king." An ominous smile crept over her red lips. "The town will be horrified to know Naboth has turned against you, and they will stone him to death—when that happens, you are to take possession of your vineyard!"

Ahab stared at his wife with his mouth agape. He blinked a few times, and a grin appeared on his lips. "My beloved! You are too ingenious!" He threw back his head and laughed. "I adore you," he whispered hoarsely.

Jezebel leaned into his kiss, and Elana recoiled in disgust. Without another glance she ran from her hiding area, covered her mouth with her hand, and cried. (The Royal Palace pg. 118)

Questions

How does Elana feel about what she heard?

_____

_____

_____

Bible Reading

It's time to open your Bible and read about Queen Jezebel. Her story is found in 1st and 2nd Kings.

Read 1 Kings 21: 4-6

Why was King Ahab upset?

_____

_____

_____

Read 1 Kings 21: 7-8

What did his wife do?

_____

_____

_____

Read 1 Kings 21: 9-11

What did she write in the letter?

_____

_____

_____

1 Kings 21:14-15

What happened to Naboth?

_____

_____

_____

Who planned Naboth's death?

_____

_____

_____

The Bible says Jezebel was an idolatrous woman and, when you read her story, you can see that she was obsessed with doing evil. She would allow nothing and nobody to stand in her way. Sadly, her husband had a weak character and did all that she said.

Personal Thoughts

What do girls your age find themselves obsessed with?

_____

_____

_____

What are some modern-day idols?

_____

_____

_____

What idols do you have in your life?

_____

_____

_____

What is one idol you want to break free from because it's causing you harm or distraction?

_____

_____

_____

Spend a few minutes in silent prayer or write out your prayer below.

Tuesday

Story

> Liz wakes up every morning at 5:30 am when her alarm goes off. She stretches and sits up, trying to come fully awake. She wishes she could curl back up in bed and go back to sleep, but she has a schedule. She reaches for her phone and checks what has happened in the world of TikTok and Instagram while she slept. She watches the videos of her favourite TikTokers and has a few laughs. Minutes crawl by and suddenly she realises one hour has passed! It's 6:30 am, and she leaves home by 7:00 am! In a dash, she rushes around, getting her things ready for school. She grabs her bag and eats a slice of toast before dashing to the bus stop where she catches the bus just in the nick of time. Puffed and bothered, she puts her headphones on and listens to music. The day already feels heavy and hectic, and it hasn't even begun!

Can you relate to Liz's dilemma? Does time also get away from you when you're on social media?

Yes   Sometimes   Always

The world is obsessed with entertainment. You only have to count the social media apps, TV shows, stories and novels you can access at the click of a mouse, and reels and videos that bombard you daily. Entertainment isn't a bad thing, but when your life is dominated with searching for entertainment and you only find joy in watching and spending hours and hours on your device—then that's an idol. Especially if it replaces your time with God.

What shows are you currently obsessed with?

_____
_____
_____

Which apps can't you live without?

_____

_____

_____

On the table put all the entertainment platforms you can think of.
For example, TikTok, Instagram, Netflix, etc.

Entertainment app/subscription, etc.	Tick all the ones you use	How long do you spend on it per week? (You can estimate.)

Which is the number one form of entertainment you enjoy most?

_____

_____

_____

Personal Thoughts

How long do you spend on private worship time or reading the bible?

_____
_____
_____

Is it more or less than your number one form of entertainment?

_____
_____
_____

Do you think your entertainment has become a god? If yes, explain. If not, explain why not.

_____
_____
_____

Pray

Spend a few minutes in silent prayer or write out your prayer below.

Wednesday

Story

> The music and chanting continued for many minutes, and just as Elana was about to leave, she watched in horror as the priestesses and priests cut their flesh with sharp objects, causing blood to come out. They splattered their blood toward their god shrine, while wailing, growling, and reciting gibberish. Ahab stood to one side and watched Jezebel, who dressed in a dark translucent gown, walked toward Baal with her arms outstretched, holding what looked like an animal. Her voice rang loud as she called different names to her god, her head thrown back as if in ecstasy. Elana felt her body tremble. This must be the witchcraft ritual Jezebel performed on a weekly basis. She had heard others speak of it, but never had she witnessed it herself. Should she be surprised? Four years ago, Queen Jezebel had been brought to the northern kingdom to be King Ahab's bride in order to strengthen the military alliance between her kingdom of Phoenicia and the kingdom of Israel. Her father, King Ethbaal, was not only a king but also the high priest of Baal. This ritual had been seeped into her since childhood. Fire spat out from the laps of the golden oxen where a gold giant bowl was laid. When Jezebel reached the top of the step and stood in front of her god, she threw her head back and shrieked the word rain over and over. Then suddenly she hurled the animal into the fire pit. She bowed low, did a distorted dance, and shouted words Elana had never heard before. Everyone cheered, and soon they broke out into unsuitable behaviour, making Elena shrink back in disgust and bolt from the obscene and disrespectful acts. Trembling, she continued running, leaving behind the smell of charred, burnt animal and smoke. (The Royal Palace pg. 98)

What would you have done in Elana's situation?

_____
_____
_____

Our idols today are not like Jezebel's statue of Baal that she kept in her garden. Idols can come in different forms.

Colossians 3:5 tells us what these things are: *"Put to death, therefore, whatever belongs to your earthly nature: <u>sexual immorality</u>, <u>impurity</u>, <u>lust</u>, <u>evil desires</u> and <u>greed</u>, <u>which is idolatry.</u>"*

This means that idols are things like:

* Sexy books
* Websites where you read sexy or steamy content
* Movies or shows
* Lustful thoughts that attack your mind
* Half-naked celebrities you keep screenshot and keep on your phone
* Inappropriate accounts you follow
* That hot guy you date or have a crush on

What idols do you struggle with?

_____

_____

_____

How do these idols take you away from God?

_____

_____

_____

Bible Reading

Write Jonah 2:8

_____
_____
_____

What does this verse mean?

_____
_____
_____

Read Matthew 6:22

What does *'the eye is the lamp of your body'* mean?

_____
_____
_____

This verse also says, *'When the eyes are healthy, your whole body is full of light.'* Explain what it means.

_____
_____
_____

Personal Thoughts

What is one thing that causes you unrest and anxiety that you are going to let go of?

_____
_____
_____

Pray

Spend a few minutes in silent prayer or write out your prayer below.

_____
_____
_____
_____
_____
_____

Thursday

Story

Jess's heart rate increases as all eyes turn on her. She feels her legs and hands shake as she holds the basketball in her hands. Her friends cheer and call out encouragement, but they aren't helping. She feels the pressure mount as her team depend on the ball she is about to shoot through the hoop so they can win. Taking a deep breath, Jess takes her position and throws the ball towards the hoop. Her heart pounds as she watches it make its way to the hoop and then...miss! She wants to dissolve into the floor and negative thoughts take hold. I'm such an idiot. What a loser. I'm worthless—not even worthy to play in this team! I'm going to quit!

Sadly, Jess has placed her identity in her team and the game.
She feels worthy and proud *only* if she scores a goal.

Questions

You might think Jess is being too harsh on herself, but have you ever been in her shoes? If not in sports, maybe in another area like art or academics? Have you ever berated yourself for something that didn't work out? What happened?

_____

_____

_____

_____

_____

Today, people place their identity in things like their social media following, what grades they achieve, sporting achievements, their looks, jobs, or their abilities and skills. They have forgotten that *'identity' is who we are in Christ*.

Why isn't it right to place your identity in things (like those mentioned)?

_____

_____

_____

Things are temporary and can change suddenly. For example, you belong to the school ensemble and play cello. Your teacher, friends, and anyone who hears you play always compliment you. You feel accomplished and proud. All your energy goes towards this instrument. However, one afternoon during physical education class, you fall and break your arm. It requires surgery and you won't be able to play until it's completely healed. That could be months away! If your identity is in being a cellist, you will be miserable for a long time.

Placing your identity in things only leads to disappointment and comparison.

What have you placed your identity on?

_____

_____

_____

If the *thing* you've placed your identity on was taken away from you right now, how would you feel?

_____

_____

_____

Placing your identity in God is <u>reliable</u>, <u>unchanging</u>, and <u>trustworthy</u>.

Look at some verses to see how God sees you and how valuable you are to Him.

Bible Reading

Read Isaiah 49:15-16

Even a parent may neglect you, or a good friend abandon you, but God promises that He won't. What has He done to show his love?

_____

_____

_____

Read 1 Peter 2:9 and fill in the blanks of the verse:

But _____ are a _____ _____, a _____ priesthood, a holy _____, God's _____ _____, that you may declare the _____ of him who called you _____ of _____ into _____ _____ light.

Draw or glue a photo of yourself in this space. Write *'My identity is in Christ'* all around the image. If you dislike drawing, write a poem or lyrics to a song of the same name.

> Your identity is based on the sacrifice Jesus made for you by dying on the cross.

When you place everything in Him, you will experience a peace that "surpasses" all understanding.

Personal Thoughts

"Idolatry happens when we take good things and make them ultimate things."

What does this quote by Timothy Keller mean?

_____

_____

_____

Pray

Spend a few minutes in silent prayer or write out your prayer below.

_____

_____

_____

_____

_____

_____

Friday

Story

Finally, after a week of celebrations, the wedding day had arrived. The day was elaborate and opulent. Ivory and gold precious stones decorated the palace corners. Tapestries enhanced with images of Baal and other gods adorned the hallways, and music played day and night. Elana could not wait for the day to be over. Kings, queens, princes, and nobles from all over the province graced the wedding of King Ahab and Princess Jezebel. For the first time, Elana caught a clear view of Princess Jezebel's face, which she had kept veiled since her arrival. The princess wore a long white gown adorned with a gold border around the hem, sleeves, and collar. They piled half her dark hair high in a Grecian hairdo, and the rest cascaded to her waist in flowy curls. Her white dress flowed to the floor, covering her bejewelled feet that Elana had helped adorn earlier that morning. A sheer white veil rested behind her crown and trailed to the floor. Her nails had been painted the colour of the moon and decorated with little gems. Her eyes had been enhanced with kohl from Egypt, and her eyelids shimmered with silver, making her amber-coloured eyes stand out.

"She looks like a goddess," Ayelet whispered.

Elana nodded. She looked incredibly beautiful but also cold and stiff, like the statues in the garden. The girls were looking from a back window that remained hidden from the guests and bridal party. They watched as King Ahab took hold of his bride, grinning like a fool and oblivious to her evil charm. A foreigner. An idolater. A Baal worshipper. And a witch who was now their new queen of Israel.

Elana sighed and said a silent prayer to Jehovah to help them all. (The Royal Palace pg. 95)

Jesus on earth

Queen Jezebel was idolatrous, volatile, and manipulative. It's a shame, because being such a woman of influence in her position as queen, she could have done a lot of good in Israel. She was unlike Jesus, who had a positive influence in this world. He was faithful to His Father and influenced others to worship God.

Bible Reading

Read the bible verses found in John 14:6-10 where Jesus is telling His disciples that He and His Father are one. One God.

God the Father

6 Jesus answered, "I am the way and the truth and the life. No one comes to the Father except through me.

7 If you really know me, you will know my Father as well. From now on, you do know him and have seen him."

8 Philip said, "Lord, show us the Father and that will be enough for us."

9 Jesus answered: "Don't you know me, Philip, even after I have been among you such a long time? Anyone who has seen me has seen the Father. How can you say, 'Show us the Father'?

10 Don't you believe that I am in the Father, and that the Father is in me? The words I say to you I do not speak on my own authority. Rather, it is the Father, living in me, who is doing his work.

Do you think God wants us to still think of Him and His Father as one God?

Yes   No   Maybe

While on earth, Jesus was the ultimate godly influence, bringing joy and peace to everyone He met. He not only talked about it, he *did* it.

Part of Isaiah 46:9 says, "I am God, and there is no other; I am God, and there is none like me."

> Remember, God is the only true God we are to worship. He sees us,
> He hears us, He loves us. There is no other God like Him.

Pray

Spend a few minutes in silent prayer or write out your prayer below!

_____
_____
_____
_____
_____
_____

Saturday/Sunday

The verse of the week: _____
_____

What did you like/dislike about the woman you studied this week?

What did you learn this week?

Why should you keep away from having idols in your life?

What's one thing you can start doing this coming week to make God your priority?

What do you need God to help you with?

Journal

Week Four

Jehosheba
Fearless Princess of Judah

"God made your spirit strong and capable of being resilient to the whirlwinds of life."

Neil L. Andersen

Monday

"The name of the LORD is a fortified tower; the righteous run to it and are safe."

Proverbs 18:10

This week: You are looking at Jehosheba, the princess who saved her nephew Joash from murder at the hands of Queen Athaliah's guards.

Personal attribute: Princess Jehosheba showed resilience. She grew up in a toxic environment, with an evil father and stepmother. Yet she rose above it all, married a priest, and despite the danger, dared to save a baby.

Definition of resilience: The ability to be happy and successful again after something difficult or bad has happened. (dictionary.cambridge.org)

Story

A sudden scream broke through the night. Jehosheba jumped and held her breath. The scream came again, closer this time. Her skin prickled as she peered over the balcony to see if she could see whoever was in trouble. She waited. Then she saw them. Her heart hammered in her chest, and perspiration wet her forehead. Drops of sweat rolled down her face. Athaliah!

Her stepmother led a procession of about fifteen priests and priestesses dancing, chanting, and playing tambourines. Jehosheba leaned over the balcony, trying to get a better look at who was screaming. Then she saw her: a young girl about her age dressed in a thin white gown being dragged by two guards. The princess frowned. What wrong could the girl have committed to deserve to be a prisoner of Athaliah?

"Let me go! Let me go," the girl pleaded.

> Suddenly Athaliah turned her head and looked up at her. Jehosheba drew in her breath and stepped back into the shadows. Her heart fluttered.
>
> Another scream pierced the darkness of the night as they passed in front of the princess's balcony. Jehosheba expected them to walk down the pathway to the prison divisions, but instead of continuing, they turned right toward the temple of Baal, which rested on a hill overlooking the city.
>
> Realisation hit Jehosheba, and her heart stopped. The girl was going to be sacrificed to Athaliah's god, Baal! She gripped the edge of the balcony, fighting a sudden dizzy spell and nausea. Hot tears fell from her face and onto the ground. What god demanded for people to be sacrificed as a gift to them? Jehosheba wiped her tears furiously. Another scream followed as the chanting got louder. Jehosheba buried her face in her hands and cried.
>
> She cried for the girl and for feeling helpless to save someone in need. Her heart hardened, and she glared at the pagan temple mocking her. How she loathed Baal. (The Royal Place pg.134)

Questions

What does the princess feel when she sees the girl going to be sacrificed?

_____

_____

_____

How would you have felt seeing the girl taken?

_____

_____

_____

Bible Reading

It's time to open your Bible and read about this princess and the family she grew up in. Her father's name was Jehoram; however, her mother's name is not mentioned in the Bible. Her half-brother was Ahaziah and her stepmother, Athaliah.

Read 2 Chronicles 21:4-5

What did her father do to secure his throne?

_____
_____
_____

Read 2 Chronicles 22:2-3

Who was Ahaziah's mother?

_____
_____
_____

What did his mother encourage him to do?

_____
_____
_____

Even though Jehosheba had grown up in a toxic environment, surrounded by people who made bad choices, she was resilient and followed another path.

Personal Thought

Do you ever complain about the family you grew up in? Explain.

_____
_____
_____
_____
_____
_____

When you face hard situations in life, how do you handle it?

_____
_____
_____

Pray

Spend a few minutes in silent prayer or write out your prayer below.

_____
_____
_____
_____
_____

Tuesday

Story

Chloe stares out of the train window, lost in her painful thoughts. She feels depressed and wishes she could find a way out of her current life situation. All her friends have a better life than she does. She shakes her head, looks down at her bruised arm, and sighs. Her father had come home drunk the night before and she woke up to the screams of her mother being beaten by him. Angrily, Chloe had run downstairs and yelled for him to stop, but he had been angry and punched her arm. He was strong, especially drunk, and she could not defend herself. Hours after he'd calmed down, he apologised, as usual, but it was too late. Chloe hated him and his volatile outbursts. She and her mum lived in constant fear but they had nowhere to go and no money of their own. Her father, CEO of an electronics company, might make millions, but he has full control over the accounts. What's the use of being rich when you live in constant pain? Chloe shakes her head as tears roll down her cheeks.

How hard is it for you to stand up to something you know is wrong?

_____
_____
_____

This or That

Highlight the ones you resonate with the most.

THIS	THAT
WHEN PROBLEMS COME MY WAY, I...	
Talk to someone about it	Keep it to myself
Feel sad but get busy doing work to forget	Feel sad and bury myself in my room
Walk off the anger and soon feel better	Get angry and punch something
Replace negative thoughts by reading uplifting quotes or the Bible	Wish I didn't exist
Have a tub of ice cream and cry	Turn to drinking alcohol to forget
Only take time off school if the situation is terrible otherwise school makes me forget as I hang out with friends	Take a few days off school until I feel better
Eat junk food for a day, then put it away	Eat junk food all week until I feel sick and throw up
Get very anxious and talk to an adult I trust	Get anxious and cry a lot—I rather not talk to anyone
Take it to God and tell him everything in my heart	Can't talk to God about it—I don't feel He listens to me
Bury myself in homework and assignments	Can't do any homework or assignments for days and fall behind in my work

Tally

This:_____ That:_____

When your score is mostly 'This': Although problems come your way, you don't let them bring you down. You have put in place some strategies that help you cope, stay resilient and not give up. Lean into the adults you trust, and surround yourself with loyal, positive friends. Find hobbies that help you cope with life during tough times and exercise! Quiet times with God are also a great way to de-stress and reset for the day. You are on a good path. Keep it up!

When your score is mostly 'That': As problems come your way, you let them bring you down. You have not yet put in place strategies or people who can help you face the tough times. It's important for you to share the load, not carry it by yourself. Maybe you don't trust many adults in your space, but there are other people you can turn to like chaplains, pastors, women leaders, or centres like Helpline that walk you through the tough times. Find people you can talk to as soon as, and whenever, you need to. It will do wonders for your soul. Quiet times with God are also a great way to de-stress and reset for the day. Don't give up! You can do this!

Were you surprised at the answer?_____

What did you discover about yourself?

_____
_____
_____

Bible Reading

Isaiah 41:10 says, So do not fear, for I am with you; do not be dismayed, for I am your God. I will strengthen you and help you; I will uphold you with my righteous right hand.

Explain what this verse means.

___

Personal Thoughts

What steps will you take to build resilience and strength in your life?

___

Pray

Spend a few minutes in silent prayer or write out your prayer below.

___

Wednesday

Story

> There was evil in the palace. Darkness loomed in every corner—it seeped through the decorated walls like honey oozing from a beehive. Jehosheba shuddered as she walked tentatively down the long hallway with its marble corridor floors. She wondered if she was overreacting, but she did not think so. The spirit of unrest and doom seemed to grow with intensity the viler Athaliah became. Jehosheba's woven sandals click-clacked too loudly for her liking. Not wanting to get caught, she continued walking on tiptoe to avoid the sound of her shoes. In the distance, she heard a door slam, followed by shouts. The princess shuddered; it was her yelling at her father again! Their shouts became louder as she got closer to her father's meeting room. She wondered what they were fighting about this time. Thinking quickly, she ran to the scroll room, which was next to her father's meeting room, and softly closed the door behind her. The dust in the room made her nose itch, and the desire to sneeze increased— she covered her mouth and nose with the sleeve of her soft, light blue linen gown and sneezed. She sighed with relief when the voices continued arguing. (The Royal Palace pg. 135)

What would you have done in Jehosheba's situation?

_____

_____

_____

It's very hard when you try to fight problems and battles on your own. God wants to help. That's why He's left you a list of 'armour' to protect you, and help you fight and defend yourself.

Bible Reading

Read Ephesians 6:10-18

List the seven pieces of armour mentioned.

1. _____
2. _____
3. _____
4. _____
5. _____
6. _____
7. _____

There is so much to cover with the Armour of God, but let's look closely at just a few important things:

Armour 1: The sword of the Spirit

The armour of a Roman soldier were mostly defensive weapons, however, the sword was the one offensive, deadly weapon that could strike and kill.

How to use the Sword of the Spirit

Using the Sword of the Spirit means that you go to God's Word (the Bible) every single day. Hebrews 4:12 says:

> "For the word of God is <u>alive and active</u>. Sharper than any double-edged sword, it <u>penetrates</u> even to <u>dividing soul and spirit, joints and marrow</u>; it judges the thoughts and attitudes of the heart."

Isn't it amazing that the Word of God is alive? It's the *ONLY* book with the power to change a person's soul and spirit. His Word fights battles and defeats foes. The rest of the Armour of God protects and keeps you safe, and includes the Helmet of Salvation, the Shield of Faith, and the Breastplate of Righteousness. When the enemy attacks what you think and believe, pick up your Bible and dive into His Word. You will fight and win because God's Word is powerful. It gives you strength and resilience!

Personal Thoughts

What step will you take this week to protect your mind from when the enemy attacks it?

_____

_____

_____

Pray

Spend a few minutes in silent prayer or write out your prayer below.

_____

_____

_____

_____

_____

_____

Thursday

Story

Emma throws her phone across the room and collapses on her bed in tears. Her boyfriend has just sent her a text breaking up with her. Her heart feels like it's shattering into a million pieces. She doesn't know how she's going to handle seeing him at school tomorrow. His text plays over and over in her mind as she lies there, crying.

I WANNA BREAK UP. I DON'T THINK WE'RE RIGHT FOR EACH OTHER. SORRY, EMMA. I DON'T WANT TO HURT YOU BUT IT'S BETTER IF WE'RE JUST FRIENDS.

They had been dating for six months and now he tells her they are not right for each other? She feels anger bubble up inside. She has a feeling that the new girl, Amber, is the cause. Josh and the new girl have been flirting with each other for weeks! Emma has tried to ignore it and not read into it, but now she knows her instincts are right. She sits up and grabs the tissue box, wiping her wet face. She needs to talk with someone. That's who she'll call! Her Aunt Sophie! She will know exactly what Emma should do.

Questions

Why is Emma hurting so much?

_____

_____

_____

Has she got the right to be crying and hurting or should she brush it off and get over it?

_____
_____
_____

What would your reaction be in her situation?

_____
_____
_____

Bible Reading

Today, you're going to look at another two pieces of God's armour that can help you be strong in any arena you face. It's crucial that you stand on your ground and practise the ability to bounce back from life's hardships. Remember, we are in a battle with the enemy, and he rejoices when we fail. Yet, Jesus wants you to win and be strong in Him.

Read Ephesian 6:14

Armour 2: The belt of Truth

Back in Roman times, soldiers wore a belt of metal and thick leather, which held their armour in place. For him to be fitted with a belt meant he was ready for action and ready to fight in battle.

How to use the belt of Truth

Reading His Word every day and learning truths means that even if the enemy tries to feed you lies and plant doubt in your mind, he won't succeed because you are aware of what God says.

The Belt of Truth "girds" you, which means it strengthens and holds you together to face life's challenges. It's a guidebook that prepares you for a life of resilience.

Bible Reading

Read Ephesians 6:18

Armour 3: Prayer

Once a Roman soldier was dressed from head to toe, with his armour firmly in place, he was ready to go into the battlefield and fight.

How to use prayer

Your battles are won on your knees. Prayer is God's power. Facing problems, pain, hurt, and other negative situations, pray. When there are things to celebrate, pray. When you need wisdom to take the next step, pray. Pray for travelling mercies. Pray over your food. Pray before bed.

Prayer is where you will hear God's voice of direction as He guides your steps.

Really, don't limit yourself to praying once a day—pray throughout your day. It's like having a silent chat with a friend—but in your mind. No one hears your thoughts, only God.

Personal Thoughts

"God made your spirit strong and capable of being resilient to the whirlwinds of life."

What does this quote by Neil L. Andersen mean?

_____

_____

_____

How can you encourage or help someone that is facing difficult times and has given up?

_____

_____

_____

Pray

Spend a few minutes in silent prayer or write out your prayer below.

_____

_____

_____

_____

_____

Friday

Story

Jehosheba ushered her friend indoors and closed the door, latching it securely in its place.

"What happened?"

Adina cried harder and buried her face in her hands. Sobs tore through her body. Jehosheba felt panic rise within her. Something terrible had happened, but Adina could barely speak. Jehosheba guided her to a seat near the door and sat with her.

"Adina, please calm yourself. Tell me what's happened!" She rubbed her friend's hands to warm them. She spoke soothing words until Adina settled.

"She killed them all."

Jehosheba frowned. "Killed?"

Adina nodded.

The princess shook her head. "Adina, I do not understand. Who killed whom?"

Adina tightened her grip. "Athaliah . . ." She took a deep, shaky breath. "Athaliah . . . has killed . . ." Her voice trailed off as tears rolled down her cheeks again.

Jehosheba froze. Killed whom?!

"When news of your brother's death came to the palace, Athaliah went crazy. Wild like a lion about to attack its prey." Adina paused, closing her eyes. "She tore her clothes and cut herself. She chanted to Baal and asked him to bring her son back."

"Oh, Adina," Jehosheba whispered.

Adina took another deep, unsteady breath. "She vowed no one would ascend to the throne but her."

> Jehosheba shook her head but did not comment, waiting for her friend to speak.
>
> "Sheba, then she... she..." Sobs tore through her body once again.
>
> The princess's heart suffered with her friend, and she rubbed her back.
>
> "She then commanded that every royal family member who would ascend to the throne was to be killed!"
>
> Jehosheba's hand went to her throat. "Oh, Adina." She felt the blood drain from her body. Her family members were dead? (The Royal Palace pg.156)

Jesus on earth

Princess Jehosheba was strong and resilient. She had faced hard times, growing up in a toxic environment, but that did not stop her from becoming a powerful woman of God. The ultimate example of resilience is *Jesus*. While on earth, He faced so much adversity, but that did not stop Him accomplishing His mission.

Bible Reading

Read the bible verses below found in Matthew 27:27-31 where Jesus is mocked by the soldiers.

The Soldiers Mock Jesus

[27] Then the governor's soldiers took Jesus into the Praetorium and gathered the whole company of soldiers around him.

[28] They stripped him and put a scarlet robe on him,

[29] and then twisted together a crown of thorns and set it on his head. They put a staff in his right hand. Then they knelt in front of him and mocked him. "Hail, king of the Jews!" they said.

[30] They spit on him and took the staff and struck him on the head again and again.

³¹ After they had mocked him, they took off the robe and put his own clothes on him. Then they led him away to crucify him.

Does God want you to be resilient when facing tough times?

Yes   No   Maybe

Next time you face a problem, what will you do to handle it?

_____

_____

_____

Jesus was the ultimate example of resilience. He not only talked about it, but He was also it.

1 Chronicles 16:11 says, "Look to the Lord and his strength; seek his face always."

Pray

Spend a few minutes in silent prayer or write out your prayer below.

_____

_____

_____

_____

_____

Saturday/Sunday

The verse of the week: _____

_____

What did you like/dislike about the woman you studied this week?

What did you learn this week?

Why do you need to be resilient?

What's one thing you can start doing this coming week to trust and depend more on God?

What do you need God to help you with?

Journal

Week Five

Esther
Courageous Queen of Persia

"Courage doesn't mean you don't get afraid. Courage means you don't let fear stop you."

Bethany Hamilton

Monday

"Have I not commanded you? Be strong and courageous. Do not be afraid; do not be discouraged, for the Lord your God will be with you wherever you go." Joshua 1:9

This week: You are looking at Esther, the young Jewish woman who became Queen and saved her people.

Personal attribute: Esther showed courage when facing the king, even though it might mean death. Courage is a wonderful trait to develop. You can face situations head-on and conquer great things.

Definition of courage: The ability to control fear and to be willing to deal with something dangerous, difficult, or unpleasant: (dictionary.cambridge.org)

Story

Esther stopped pacing and walked to Hathach to retrieve the paper he held out to her. This must be what the two maids were talking about the other day, and Haman's meeting in secret with those men was definitely about the decree. Anger boiled inside her. With trembling fingers, she unrolled the paper and read every word. Tears filled her eyes and they silently rolled down her cheeks and neck.

"Oh, Mordecai," she whispered. "What can I do to help you?"

"My lady?"

Esther turned her wet face to her servant.

"Mordecai also sends a personal message for you."

"What is it?"

"He is begging you to go to King Xerxes and plea for mercy for him and for all the Jewish people, so the decree can be eliminated."

Esther gulped. Mordecai did not know what he asked. It was forbidden for her to see the king without being summoned by him. If she went to see him uninvited, he would have her killed!

"Hathach, that is impossible. Unless the king calls for me, I cannot see him. I would be put to death immediately. It has been thirty days since I last visited him."

Hathach nodded. "I explained that to Mordecai."

"What was his reply?" Esther wiped her eyes with the edge of her long, transparent veil.

"He said that you should not think that because you are in the king's house, you alone of all the Jews will escape. For if you remain silent, deliverance will arise from another place. However, you and your father's house will perish. And who knows but that you have come to a royal position for such a time as this?"

Esther's head spun around at the words of Mordecai. She felt like she had just been gently slapped across the face. Her lips trembled and her heart hammered. He spoke the truth. Everything he said was correct. God had sent her to save her people. She turned her back to Hathach and tried to make sense of her swirling thoughts. Was she able to save her people? Had she been sent for such a time as this, as Mordecai stated? What could she do? (The Royal Palace pg.221)

Questions

How does Esther feel when she gets the message from Mordecai?

_____

_____

_____

What would you have done in her situation?

___

Bible Reading

It's time to open your Bible and read about Esther. Her story is found in the Book of Esther.

Read Esther 2:7

Who was Esther?

___

Read Esther 2:1-4

Why was she taken to the palace?

___

Read Esther 3:8-9

What happened when she was living in the palace?

Personal Thoughts

Do you believe you have courage?

Is courage something you have thought about before?

Is courage something you would like to develop?

Spend a few minutes in silent prayer or write out your prayer below.

Tuesday

Story

> Isla looks in the mirror and cringes at her reflection. Her sparkly, 'can't-breathe-or-bend-over-in-that dress' glows from every angle as the light hits each sequin. Her massive heels make her feel like she will tumble over at any moment. Light brown curls cascade to her waist and her lips look bee-stung and swollen, ten times bigger under her gold lipstick. She touches her face and winces. If her dad sees her dressed like this, he will flip! Why is she letting Hailey push her into dressing like her, anyway? Yeah, Hailey is gorgeous and popular, but Isla doesn't feel like herself in these clothes. She glances over at Hailey, who finishes putting on her lipstick, and suddenly feels little bubbles of anger rise up inside. She is done! No way is she going to let someone think for her. With a frustrated grunt, Isla kicks off her shoes and turns to face Hailey.

Why was Isla so upset?

_____
_____
_____

When does she show courage?

_____
_____
_____

What would you have done in Isla's situation?

_____

_____

_____

Word Search—Find all the words of this Bible verse.

Some great verses in the Bible talk about courage. Below is a word search. Find the words, then look up the verse in the bible and write it below.

```
E  P  I  U  A  N  D  R  A  M  F  G  T  I  M  I  D  V
Z  O  S  S  E  Y  L  C  C  D  D  R  N  N  U  T  G  Q
U  W  V  H  M  F  O  R  K  P  D  L  I  E  S  N  T  Y
V  E  V  S  E  L  F  D  I  S  C  I  P  L  I  N  E  P
F  R  N  G  H  S  L  Q  I  N  K  K  G  A  V  E  S  M
D  A  E  I  V  M  E  N  O  T  O  L  E  U  M  U  S  T
E  O  M  V  E  L  Q  V  G  Q  P  J  C  M  D  O  P  E
N  F  E  E  M  A  K  E  E  L  E  M  M  B  S  N  I  Y
K  T  D  S  O  B  T  L  G  N  O  T  I  A  Z  E  R  T
G  O  D  O  C  U  F  H  Y  N  W  V  Z  R  X  S  I  V
G  W  D  M  L  T  S  A  E  S  V  I  E  X  L  F  T  D
R  G  F  H  P  L  T  E  N  T  I  M  O  T  H  Y  H  C
```

Find the following words.

AND	MAKE	TIMID
BUT	NOT	TIMOTHY
DOES	ONE	US
FOR	POWER	
GAVE	SELF-DISCIPLINE.	
GIVES	SEVEN	
GOD	SPIRIT	
LOVE	THE	

Write 2 Timothy 1:7 in the space.

_____

_____

_____

God gives us courage. He doesn't want us to shy away from difficult things, but stand up for what we believe. As this verse says, He has given us POWER to do this, and we are to do it with LOVE.

Personal Thoughts

What is one thing you would love to do but feel too afraid to have a go?

_____

_____

_____

How can you become more courageous if that is something you are lacking?

_____

_____

_____

Pray

Spend a few minutes in silent prayer or write out your prayer below.

_____

_____

_____

_____

_____

_____

Wednesday

Story

Esther knew she couldn't do this alone. She needed help. She knew what she had to do. Taking a deep breath, she walked to the eunuch and stepped closer to him. Her jewels jingled with each movement.

"Tell Mordecai to gather all the Jews who are in Susa and to fast and pray for me. Tell him not to drink or eat for three days, night or day. My maids and I will fast as well. When this is done, I will go to the king even if it is against the law."

Fear flashed in Hathach's eyes. "My queen! That means death!"

Esther rubbed her hands together, trying hard to keep her composure. Tears filled her eyes and silently spilled down her face and onto her elaborate afternoon gown covered in gold and jewellery. "If I perish, I perish!"

Seeing the queen's determination, Hathach bowed and left the room to deliver the message.

Unable to hold her composure any longer, Esther crumbled onto the nearest garden bench and sobbed.

The next day, Esther spoke to her maids and instructed them regarding her fasting commitment for the next three days. No one asked questions, but the fear everyone felt was evident. Their queen could die if she made an uninvited appearance to see King Xerxes.

That night, as Esther looked out the window at the flickering lights of the stars, her heart ached. The heaviness she carried was intense, but she could not let that consume her thoughts. She had to hold every thought captive, with God's help. She closed her eyes and prayed—nothing else mattered for the next three days but to be in silent communion with the God of Abraham. Her life was in His hands. (The Royal Palace pg.221)

What would you have done in Queen Esther's situation?

_____
_____
_____

Have you ever experienced a time you had to be courageous?

Yes   No

Explain what happened.

_____
_____
_____

Has anybody ever done something courageous for you?

_____
_____
_____

Who was the person?

_____
_____
_____

What did they do?

___

How did you feel afterward?

___

Bible Reading

Look at the following verses to see what the Bible says about being courageous or having courage.

Deuteronomy 31:6

"Be strong and courageous. Do not be afraid or terrified because of them, for the Lord your God goes with you; he will never leave you nor forsake you."

God says you need to be strong and_____?

Why should you be unafraid?

___

Who goes before you?

When will God leave you?

There's a nice verse in Psalm 56:3 that says:

"When I am afraid, I put my trust in you."

What does this verse mean?

Personal Thoughts

What is one courageous thing you can do today?

Pray

Spend a few minutes in silent prayer or write out your prayer below.

_____
_____
_____
_____
_____
_____

Thursday

Story

Zoe gulps and stares at her teacher like she has suddenly grown two heads. "Zoe... Zoe? You okay?" Mrs Omar tilts her head to one side and looks at her.

Zoe blinks and shakes her head. "Sorry, umm... What did you want me to do?"

"I would like you and Jess to welcome the parents to the Art exhibit and give them a bit of an intro on what your class has been doing this semester."

"But, Miss, that completely freaks me out! I don't like talking in public, especially to adults!" Zoe feels her voice elevate a few pitches, feels her heart thumping in her chest, and suddenly, cannot breathe properly. No way. I can't! she thinks.

"Zoe, you are one of my best Art students and I would really like parents to hear what the experience has been like from a student's (not a teacher's!) point of view." Mrs. Omar fixes her big hoop yellow earrings and continues talking. "You need to believe you can do this. I know you can!"

Zoe shifts her art book to her left hand and sighs. Mrs. Omar is her favourite teacher, and she doesn't want to let her down, but she knows she can never talk in front of an audience. How can she get out of this?

"Please, Zoe, think about it and let me know by tomorrow. I can help you write your intro and practice with you and Jess." Mrs. Omar pauses. "Please. Think about it?"

Taking a deep breath, Zoe nods and gives her teacher a thumbs up. "Sure, I'll think about it." She swallows the lump in her throat and bolts out of the art room and into the cool air.

Questions

What do you think Zoe's answer will be?

_____

_____

_____

Does she believe she can do it?

_____

_____

_____

Who believes in her?

_____

_____

_____

Bible Reading

Write Joshua 1:9

_____

_____

_____

Explain what this verse means.

_____

_____

_____

Read Psalm 34:4

"I sought the Lord, and he answered me; he delivered me from all my fears."

What happens when you call to God?

_____

_____

_____

How will trusting Him help your fear?

_____

_____

_____

Personal Thoughts

"Courage doesn't mean you don't get afraid. Courage means you don't let fear stop you."

What does this quote by Bethany Hamilton mean?

_____

_____

_____

Pray

Spend a few minutes in silent prayer or write out your prayer below.

_____

_____

_____

_____

_____

_____

_____

Friday

Story

Hathach opened the grand, heavy golden doors to the inner court of the king's house, and they entered the viewing room, which was decorated with glazed bricks depicting winged bulls, sphinxes, and griffins. Esther's heart beat fast. She knew that at the end of that corridor, there would be another room with the door open, and the king would be seated on his throne. The time had arrived. Hathach slowed his pace as they approached the gold door decorated with sphinxes. He turned to look at her with deeply sad eyes.

"Queen Esther." He moved out of the way so she could proceed.

Esther touched his arm briefly and walked past him to her impending doom.

As she walked the last few steps, all she could hear was the sound of her jewellery rattling at her every pace. She came to a stop at the open door and saw the king sitting upon his royal throne facing the entrance. It looked like he was in a meeting with those around him.

Suddenly the king leaned forward with eyes wide. "Esther?"

At the mention of her name, the soldiers lining the entrance all the way to the throne rushed with spears toward her and blocked her from going inside. A little moan escaped her lips, and she eagerly waited for God to act. Even though she felt afraid, she trusted Him. (The Royal Palace pg. 224)

Jesus on earth

Queen Esther risked it all. In those days, if you were not invited to see the king and went without his welcome, he was within his rights to kill you. Esther knew her life hung in the balance. Yet even though she was afraid, she faced the situation head-on. "If I perish, I perish," she said. Over history, there has been one example of ultimate courage: *Jesus*. While on earth, Jesus faced so many challenges, each one head-on. The hardest one he had to face was His death.

Bible Reading

Read the story below found in Matthew 22:39-46 where Jesus showed great courage as He faced death.

Jesus Prays on the Mount of Olives

³⁹ Jesus went out as usual to the Mount of Olives, and his disciples followed him.

⁴⁰ On reaching the place, he said to them, "Pray that you will not fall into temptation."

⁴¹ He withdrew about a stone's throw beyond them, knelt down and prayed,

⁴² "Father, if you are willing, take this cup from me; yet not my will, but yours be done."

⁴³ An angel from heaven appeared to him and strengthened him.

⁴⁴ And being in anguish, he prayed more earnestly, and his sweat was like drops of blood falling to the ground.

⁴⁵ When he rose from prayer and went back to the disciples, he found them asleep, exhausted from sorrow.

⁴⁶ "Why are you sleeping?" he asked them. "Get up and pray so that you will not fall into temptation."

Do you think God wants you to be courageous in life?

Yes   No   Maybe

What usually gives you the courage to face problems and keep going forward each day?

_____

_____

_____

> Jesus was the ultimate example of courage when He faced death for you and me. He not only spoke of courage, but He was also courageous!

Luke 23:46 says, Jesus called out with a loud voice, "Father, into your hands I commit my spirit." When he had said this, he breathed his last.

Pray

Spend a few minutes in silent prayer or write out your prayer below.

_____

_____

_____

_____

_____

_____

Saturday/Sunday

The verse of the week: _____
_____

What did you like/dislike about the woman you studied this week?

What did you learn this week?

Why should you be courageous?

What's one courageous thing you can start doing this coming week?

What do you need God to help you with?

Journal

Week Six

Salome

Seductress Princess of Jerusalem

"Those who follow the crowd usually get lost in it."

Rick Warren

Monday

"Finally, be strong in the Lord and in his mighty power. Put on the full armor of God, so that you can take your stand against the devil's schemes."
Ephesians 6:10-11

This week: You are looking at Princess Salome who danced for King Herod, her stepfather, and asked for the head of John the Baptist. The Bible doesn't give us the name of Salome—it only says Herodia's daughter. However, historians have uncovered that her name was Salome.

Personal attribute: The princess was influenced and pressured by her mother to do a certain dance and ask for John's head. This week, you're going to learn about negative peer pressure and how being influenced by others can cause harm to you and your friends.

Definition of peer pressure: The strong influence of a group, especially of children, on members of that group to behave as everyone else does or the pressure that you feel to behave in a certain way because your friends or people in your group expect it. (dictionary.cambridge.org)

In this week's study, you will look at parts of Princess Salome's story and short stories of girls your age.

Story

The next few days were busy for Salome as she continued arduous hours of twirling, pirouetting, and swaying. Tabina was a rigorous teacher and made her work too hard. Salome was not used to so much physical activity; princesses usually spent a lot of time indoors and entertaining. This was new to her. Some days, her mother would come in and watch her perform. She whispered instructions to Tabina, who voiced them to Salome. Salome grunted in frustration but remained silent. She knew her mother would slap her if she questioned her actions. Her hand went to her face as if the sting of her mother's handprint still ached on her cheek.

"Much better, Princess Salome. Much better." Tabina moved around Salome as she danced. "Sway your hips. You have curves that are envied by many women. Use them accordingly."

Salome tried again. This time Tabina approved.

"Remember, Princess, you must captivate your audience. Especially the men in the room."

Salome winced.

"Now, start again from the beginning. Perform to perfection," Tabina commanded.

Determination took over and Salome asserted she would show Tabina that she could do it. If Tabina saw her perform to her satisfaction, then she would tell Herodias and maybe let her have a few days off. (The Royal Palace pg. 249)

Questions

How does the princess feel at this dance routine her mother has got her doing?

_____

_____

_____

What would you have done in her situation?

___

Bible Reading

The Herod's were known for their evil and cruelty. Herod the Tetrarch was the son of Herod the Great who commanded all babies be killed in Baby Jesus' time.

Read Mark 6:21

What did Herod do on his birthday?

___

Read Mark 6:22-24

What did Princess Salome do for the king?

___

What did Herod promise his stepdaughter?

What did Salome do when she heard the king's offer?

What does her attitude *'to go to her mother'* tell you about her character?

Personal Thoughts

Do you rely on other people to tell you what to do? Why or why not?

Write about a time you ever felt pressured to do something you didn't want to do.

What can happen if you give in to negative peer pressure or influence?

Pray

Spend a few minutes in silent prayer or write out your prayer below.

Tuesday

Story

Faye shakes her head. Everything inside her screams "No!" But she does not want to look like a goody-two-shoes in front of her friends. She doesn't have a choice—does she? Her friends keep pushing her to drink and smoke. There are no adults at home, so they can do anything they want. She feels torn between what her friend is doing or listening to her parents. What will they say if they find out she has vaped and is now thinking of drinking alcohol? She cringes. She has grown up in a strong Christian home. Drinking and smoking have never been part of her life. And now, here she is at her friend's 15th birthday party, and she's considering taking her first drink. Joel hands her the cup with the alcoholic mixture. With trembling fingers, but while still trying to look cool, she takes a large gulp. Her throat burns, and her eyes sting and water. Her whole body feels on fire. The sensation is strange, but the forbidden act excites her. Should she drink another? She nods and asks Joel to give her another shot. She might as well go all the way.

What is peer pressure?

Why do you feel a need to fit in?

What kind of peer pressure have you experienced at school or church?

Have you ever vaped or drunk alcohol? What happened and why did you want to do it?

How did you feel afterward?

Did anyone find out?

Would you do it again? Why or why not?

_____

_____

_____

What does the Bible say about doing whatever our bodies desire? Open your Bible to Galatians 5:16-21 and match the Bible verses below to find out.

17. and envy; drunkenness, orgies, and the like. I warn you, as I did before, that those who live like this will not inherit the kingdom of God.

20. The acts of the flesh are obvious: sexual immorality, impurity and debauchery;

16. But if you are led by the Spirit, you are not under the law.

19. idolatry and witchcraft; hatred, discord, jealousy, fits of rage, selfish ambition, dissensions, factions

18. So I say, walk by the Spirit, and you will not gratify the desires of the flesh.

21. For the flesh desires what is contrary to the Spirit, and the Spirit what is contrary to the flesh. They are in conflict with each other, so that you are not to do whatever you want.

Read the verse out loud in order: 16-21.

At times, you will feel drawn to do things that aren't good or good for you. You'll want to fit in or experiment. However, it's important to stand strong in your faith because none of the acts of the flesh help you in any way. They are more likely to hurt you or others.

Personal Thoughts

Matthew 26:41 says *"Watch and pray so that you will not fall into temptation. The spirit is willing, but the flesh is weak."*

What does this verse mean?

_____

_____

_____

It's never too late to start again. If you feel like you've let yourself down—unworthy—because you've done any of the above things, or are still doing it, you can start again.

God loves you and wants you to come to Him just as you are. Everything He says is to save, not ruin, your life. He wants you to be healthy, strong, and well.

Pray

Spend a few minutes in silent prayer or write out your prayer below.

_____

_____

_____

_____

_____

_____

Wednesday

Story

Salome rushed to her mother's side. "I do not know what to ask for?" She felt her hands sweat. How humiliating to have the king and his guests waiting for her answer!

"Come, my petal, tell me the desires of your heart!" Herod hollered.

The crowd roared with him.

Salome turned back to her mother and waited for her to reply. She watched her mother's face flash with satisfaction as she leaned over and whispered in her ear, "Ask for the head of John the Baptist."

Salome blinked. Had she heard correctly?

"What did you say?" she asked.

"Ask for the head of John the Baptist."

This time she heard her clearly, and her heart thundered in her chest.

"John the Baptist?" she choked, her hand going to her throat.

Salome was astonished. She did not understand the hidden revenge in her mother's heart.

"No!" she said between clenched teeth. "I will not!"

She began to shake, and sweat broke through her body. She could not ask for such an inhumane act to take place. No! She shook her head.

"I will not, Mother. No."

> Her mother moved closer to Salome and whispered venomously, "Ask for John's head, or I will ask for yours."
>
> Salome's head shot up. The wicked look in her eyes made Salome tremble. She was serious.
>
> "Hurry, Daughter, Herod awaits your decision." A smirk danced on her mother's lips.
>
> Muted by her mother's action, Salome walked backward, watching Herodias's face the whole time. She could not tear her eyes away from her. (The Royal Palace pg. 259)

What would you have done in Salome's situation?

Who was pressuring her?

Do you think the decision she made was easy or hard? Why?

What are some things friends can pressure you to do? List 3 to 5 things.

_____
_____
_____
_____
_____
_____

Sometimes your friends will attempt to influence or force you to change the way you talk, walk, the way you dress, and do your hair. There is nothing wrong with wanting a little makeover, redo your hair or get new clothes; however, it's important to do it for *you*. Don't let anyone tell you that you're not good enough the way you are or the way you look.

> God created you, perfectly you. He wants to see you thrive as yourself, not as a copy of someone else.

Bible Reading

What do the following verses say about who you are to God? Open your Bible and write what you find in the space provided.

Write Psalm 139:14

_____
_____
_____

Write Ephesians 2:10

_____
_____
_____

Write Isaiah 49:16

_____
_____
_____

Next time someone tries to influence you to be more like them, remember who you belong to. Copy Him instead.

In Philippians 4:13, there's a great verse that says, *"I can do all this through him who gives me strength."*

To have victory you need to study God's word daily and pray.

Personal Thought

How loved are you by God?

_____
_____
_____

Spend a few minutes in silent prayer or write out your prayer below.

___

___

___

___

___

___

Thursday

Story

Isabelle gasps when Josh slams the door of the school sports shed.

"Isabelle, I think you're so beautiful." He reaches for a strand of her blonde hair and slips it behind her ear. She gulps, and her heart hammers in her chest. She likes Josh a lot and can't believe he is telling her she is beautiful! How could the cutest, most popular boy in year 11 be interested in her?

He stares at Isabelle's lips. In what feels like slow motion, he leans in to her, pinning her against the door. His eyes close and lips part. Isabelle's body trembles, her mouth feels dry, and she wonders if she's about to pass out. She wants to kiss him so badly! She's dreamed of this moment! Slowly, she moves forward and their lips touch. Electricity shoots through her body as their kiss intensifies. Josh's kisses move from her lips to her cheeks and then to her neck. His hands roam her body, and she stiffens. Okay, he's kissed her, but now he's touching her in places that are private and make her feel uncomfortable.

She puts her hands against his chest and pushes him off.

"Josh," she breathes hard, unable to talk properly.

Josh laughs, moves her hands away, and starts kissing her again. "Relax Issi," he whispers.

With force, she pushes him back. "Josh, stop! What are you doing?"

He licks his lips and stares at her in confusion. "I thought you wanted me like I want you!"

She shakes her head. "I'm not ready to do this." She exhales, placing a trembling palm against the pulse that is going wild in her neck.

> He pales, then reddens. "You're kidding, right?" He says incredulously.
>
> Isabelle's eyes fill with tears. "I can't Josh. What would God think?"
>
> Josh draws back. His handsome face darkens. "God? Are you for real? Don't be such a nun!"
>
> "You're a Christian, too! We shouldn't have sex."
>
> For a minute Isabelle thinks he's going to hit her. She holds her breath. *God help me.* Josh glares, then bangs the door open with a fist. He turns and scowls on his way out: "Good luck ever getting a guy. Maybe you should go live in a convent!" He spits out these last words before disappearing out the door.
>
> Isabelle exhales and buries her face in her hands. She wants to cry.

It would have been so easy for Isabelle to lose her virginity to Josh, and it took a lot of guts to stand up and say no.

Questions

Think for a moment about you and your crush kissing. He wants to sleep with you. What would you do?

_____

_____

_____

What would be the consequences of having sex early? Make a list of at least three consequences.

_____

_____

_____

When Isabelle says, *"What would God think?"* what did she mean?

_____

_____

_____

Sex itself isn't wrong—God created it in the Garden of Eden! The beginning of Genesis 1:28 says, *"God blessed them and said to them, 'Be fruitful and increase in number; fill the earth and subdue it....'"*

See, God gave Adam and Eve a command to increase in numbers, and they would do this by having babies. So, what's the problem with sex before marriage?

There's something sacred about marriage, about going on your honeymoon with your husband—for the first time being together. It's special, giving yourself to him completely, with God's blessing, and without hiding it from parents or anyone else because you are now husband and wife.

> Every time you have sex with another guy, it's like leaving a little piece of your body and emotion with him—something you can never take back.

Sexual acts are not only sleeping with someone. What about sexting? Think for a minute before sending nude photos of yourself to guys you like or to someone who requests them. What would happen if those photos leak, or if he sends them to someone in your school or church?

There is no rush to be sexually active. Now is the time to grow and become the woman God created you to be. Respect your body and make it into a true temple of God. One day, God will send you the right man, the one you will marry and have children with. It's worth the wait and you'll enjoy being with your husband and preparing your little family for heaven.

Bible Reading

Read 1 Corinthians 16:13.

Explain what this verse means.

_____

_____

_____

What will you do to grow strong in God, so that when temptations come you can stand firm?

_____

_____

_____

Personal Thoughts

"Those who follow the crowd usually get lost in it."

What does this quote by Rick Warren mean?

_____
_____
_____

What steps can you take so you don't get lost when following everyone else?

_____
_____
_____

Pray

Spend a few minutes in silent prayer or write out your prayer below.

_____
_____
_____
_____
_____

Friday

Story

Salome took a deep breath and rang out the words. "I want the head of John the Baptist."

The uncontrolled mirth ceased, and an ominous silence settled over every single guest. All Salome could hear was the thundering of her own heart. Salome watched his face flicker with emotions. Although he was drunk, he understood the severity of the request. His eyes roamed the room until they settled on Herodias. Salome watched him clench and unclench his fists as he battled the demand. Frustrated, he hurled his cup to one side and let it shatter on a wall covered in tapestry. Red wine trickled down and onto the marble floor. A pool of red formed on the ground, and Salome grimaced. Red, like blood. John's blood. She turned her attention back to Herod, who was watching her intently. She wanted to scream and yell that she did not want that request, but the look on her mother's face prevented her from it.

Finally, she watched Herod descend the stairs until he was towering over her. He lifted her chin with one of his fingers. "Your request is my command!" He whirled around and back up the steps, his cape flowing behind him. He clicked his fingers to the soldiers at the door, and they scurried in. "Get me the head of John the Baptist, now!"

The two Roman soldiers dressed in their authoritative uniform saluted and tore out of the room.

Salome covered her face and tried to process what had just happened. The king, still standing in the same spot, looked numb and confused.

Salome's eyes travelled to her mother, who was the only one grinning from ear to ear. Salome felt sick. (The Royal Palace pg.261)

Jesus on earth

Sadly, Princess Salome was pressured into doing things she did not want to do. Her mother had a massive influence over her life, and she found it hard to say "No." The *only* person never influenced by another person is *Jesus*. The Pharisees tried pushing him into becoming someone He wasn't, but Jesus stood His ground. He was even pressured by the Devil to do things He didn't want to do.

Bible reading

Read the story below found in Luke 4:1-13 where the enemy pressures Jesus in the desert.

Jesus Is Tested in the Wilderness

1 Jesus, full of the Holy Spirit, left the Jordan and was led by the Spirit into the wilderness,

2 where for forty days he was tempted by the devil. He ate nothing during those days, and at the end of them he was hungry.

3 The devil said to him, "If you are the Son of God, tell this stone to become bread."

4 Jesus answered, "It is written: 'Man shall not live on bread alone.

5 The devil led him up to a high place and showed him in an instant all the kingdoms of the world.

6 And he said to him, "I will give you all their authority and splendor; it has been given to me, and I can give it to anyone I want to.

7 If you worship me, it will all be yours."

8 Jesus answered, "It is written: 'Worship the Lord your God and serve him only.'

9 The devil led him to Jerusalem and had him stand on the highest point of the temple. "If you are the Son of God," he said, "throw yourself down from here.

10 For it is written: "'He will command his angels concerning you to guard you carefully;

11 they will lift you up in their hands, so that you will not strike your foot against a stone.'

12 Jesus answered, "It is said: 'Do not put the Lord your God to the test.'

13 When the devil had finished all this tempting, he left him until an opportune time.

Jesus stood strong and didn't fall for the Devil's peer pressure!

Do you think Jesus understands how hard it is to avoid temptation and the pressure from friends to do the wrong thing?

Yes   No   Maybe

What temptation or peer pressure do you find hard to resist?

_____

_____

_____

Jesus is the ultimate example of what it's like not to fall for peer pressure. He not only talked about being strong, but He was also strong.

Psalm 50:15 says, ...and call on me in the day of trouble; I will deliver you, and you will honor me.

Pray

Spend a few minutes in silent prayer or write out your prayer below.

Saturday/Sunday

The verse of the week: _____

_____

What did you like/dislike about the woman you studied this week?

What did you learn this week?

Why should you stand strong and not be negatively influenced by others?

What's one thing you can start doing this coming week to get closer to God?

What do you need God to help you with?

Journal

Answer Page

Here are the answers to the activities in the book.

Week 1—Tuesday   Quiz answer varies.

Week 2—Tuesday   Fill in the gap Acts 17:27 (NIV)
God did this so that they would seek him and perhaps reach out for him and find him, though he is not far from any one of us.

Week 3—Tuesday   answers vary

Week 4—Tuesday   answers vary

Week 5—Tuesday   word search

```
. P . U A N D . . . . . T I M I D .
. O . S . . . . . . . . . U . . . .
. W . . F O R . . . . . . S . . . .
. E . S E L F D I S C I P L I N E .
. R . G . S . . . . . G A V E . . .
D . . I . . E N O T . . . . . . S .
. O . V . . V . . . . . . . . O P .
. . E E M A K E E L . . . . . N I .
. . . S . B T . . N O . . . . E R .
G O D . . U . H . . . V . . . . I .
. . . . . . T S . E . . . E . . . T .
. . . . . . . . . T I M O T H Y . .
```

Word directions and start points are formatted: (Direction, X, Y)

AND (SE,3,8)
BUT (S,9,1)
DOES (E,5,10)
FOR (E,12,6)
GAVE (S,11,6)
GIVES (S,5,2)
GOD (E,15,1)
LOVE (S,7,3)
MAKE (SE,14,7)
NOT (SE,16,3)
ONE (SE,2,3)
POWER (S,13,5)
SELF-DISCIPLINE. (E,3,11)
SEVEN (E,6,8)
SPIRIT (E,4,7)
THE (S,12,7)
TIMID (S,18,5)
TIMOTHY (E,8,12)
US (SE,2,5)

Week 6—Tuesday   Match the verse with the number.

21. and envy; drunkenness, orgies, and the like. I warn you, as I did before, that those who live like this will not inherit the kingdom of God.

19. The acts of the flesh are obvious: sexual immorality, impurity and debauchery;

18. But if you are led by the Spirit, you are not under the law.

20. idolatry and witchcraft; hatred, discord, jealousy, fits of rage, selfish ambition, dissensions, factions

16. So I say, walk by the Spirit, and you will not gratify the desires of the flesh.

17. For the flesh desires what is contrary to the Spirit, and the Spirit what is contrary to the flesh. They are in conflict with each other, so that you are not to do whatever you want.

About the Author

M.E. Mayorga is known to everyone by her middle name, Esther. She loves reading and writing books. If she could have her own library, she would.

Esther is the cohost of two popular podcasts: one for children called Car Ride Stories for GIGI Kids and one for teen girls called GIGI Teen Radio.

She enjoys cowriting with her younger sister Stephanie, and together they are creating an exciting Christian series for teen girls called Charlotte Bay Girls.

She lives in sunny Brisbane, Australia, and is looking forward to moving to the countryside one day, where she can find more creative inspiration in the beauty of the rolling hills and the quiet.

You can connect with Esther at www.gigistorylibrary.com.au or on Instagram @gigi_teen_girl, or you can email her at writegigi5@gmail.com. She will definitely reply to your email!

PS: GIGI stands for "Gorgeous in God's Image."

www.ingramcontent.com/pod-product-compliance
Lightning Source LLC
Chambersburg PA
CBHW061806290426
44109CB00031B/2948